"[*Chrome Valley*] dives deep into the experience of Black girlhood and womanhood in America, with [Mahogany L.] Browne reflecting on everything from her own maternal lineage to the yearning-laden pleasure of young friendship to the true meaning of inherited trauma and the power that it can hold to shape our lives." —Emma Specter, *Vogue*

"With great compassion and fury, Browne shows how survival has become an act of defiance." —Shannon Carlin, *Time*

"Mahogany L. Browne has long established herself to be one of the great living poets. But what is clear upon reading her luminous new collection is that she is a master historian as well: of the heart, of lineage, of the griefs and joys that come with Blackness, girlhood, and motherhood in this country—and all their intersections." —Hala Alyan, author of *The Arsonists' City*

"Browne's moving latest commemorates the struggles of Black women, drawing on episodes from her life and stories from family members. While these poems vividly relay the threat of violence ('the gun answers the door before / anyone ever knocks'), they also crystallize moments of intimacy.... These are powerful poems of witness and reckoning."

—*Publishers Weekly*, starred review

"From a palindrome to prose poems, this electric and much-anticipated collection by Browne, a prolific writer, examines Black girlhood and womanhood, desire, friendship, and migration.

My mind keeps circling 'Stumble Lovely,' a title so beautiful I envision it tattooed obvious and tender places to be carried close always."
　　　　　　　　　　　　　　　　　　　—Connie Pan, *Book Riot*

"Mahogany L. Browne's poetry is the outstretched arm holding innocence in its seat as we approach a sharp, violent red light. It is an honor to continue to have her language in the driver's seat, telling us where to look, and when to close our eyes."
　　　　　　　　　　—Camonghne Felix, author of *Build Yourself a Boat*,
　　　　　　　　　　　　　　　longlisted for the National Book Award

"Mahogany L. Browne's legacy is one of generosity, a legacy that once again shines through in *Chrome Valley*, which acts as a booklong ode, a love song to both place and people, so rich in image and narrative clarity that the place could be your place. And, for our folks, the people could be your people."
　　　　　　　　　　—Hanif Abdurraqib, author of *A Little Devil in America:*
　　　　　　　　　　　　　　　Notes in Praise of Black Performance

"If you want to know what it feels like to truly celebrate the magic of Black womanhood, Mahogany L. Browne's *Chrome Valley* should be your starting point. . . . Imagine the lyrics to a ratched opera, Jesus meeting his maker—a Black woman—and you will fall deep inside this vivacious, tender, high-voltage collection. . . . *Chrome Valley* is not just a book; it's a destination, a practice, a memory, a corner of deliverance."
　　　　　　　　　　—Willie Perdomo, State Poet of New York and
　　　　　　　　　　　　　　　　　author of *The Crazy Bunch*

CHROME VALLEY

CHROME VALLEY

POEMS

MAHOGANY L. BROWNE

LIVERIGHT PUBLISHING CORPORATION

A Division of W. W. Norton & Company

INDEPENDENT PUBLISHERS SINCE 1923

To Elsie Jean, My forever Matriarch

CONTENTS

CHROME VALLEY

HOMER, LOUISIANA

i.

When you are a Black writer in America:
it gets harder to ignore the bodies.

To step over the nameless namesakes
and point apparatus to the sun.

They say writing about the almost dead only gets harder.
My grandma sighs "pray for them baby."

I think "God! Is this the fight?
To be Black and beautiful and breathing?"

ii.

When I say freedom
What I mean is American flag
knotted in the spine & ripped from the root
When I say root
What I mean is Detroit Red
What I mean is Malcolm X
What I mean is Barack Obama

What I mean is history repeating itself
What I mean is history rewriting itself
What I mean is apple pie
with a slave owner on the side

iii.

you know you Black
when no one wants to talk
about how your blk hair kink
up into clean circles
how they white ass bathroom floor
don't hide the coiled curls
like ya mama's tan tiles do
so you crawl on all fours
with toilet paper tap water damp around your knuckles
so no one notices
that you notice
that your kitchen is as nappy
as they told you it was
& here you be
black ass grown ass woman
on all fours
who stay saying her afro is beautiful

who been saying she love her black
who keep saying she ain't
afraid

iv.

When I say root
What I mean is Fannie Lou Hamer
What I mean is size 10 & no laces
What I mean is history repeating itself
What I mean is history rewriting itself
What I mean is apple pie
with a prison warden on the side

When I say side
What I mean is handcuffed & kicked,
stripped & water hosed,
bare & ass & thighs debated on its firm
during prime time
When I say prime time
What I mean is ratchet opera,
hood rat antics turned fabulous,
turned appropriated for *honey*
boo boo chile consumption

When I say consumption
What I mean is—O, say can you see
Miley Cyrus & Raven-Symoné got a TV show called
America Ain't Got No Talent

But we twerk & shake & can sale anything
on top a black woman's ass
& turn it solid gold

v.

Your people come from Homer, Louisiana

& all you know is a tale of the night when

Your grandpa Lester
stole your great grandma Octavia
& great grandpa Nell
from the spitshine sharecropper
into a dirt-poor freedom up North.

How they threatened to lynch him
& his dog before daybreak,
how his slick mouth was a gunshot wound
waiting.

& you never heard him whistle *Dixie* no.

Only his southern twang riding high in Oakland, CA
brown cracked fists shield his eyes from the top of the porch
every morning like prayer
—& watch the sun rise

THE BLK(EST) NIGHT 1993

jesus came to the crib
saw the blk(est) girl w/her box braids
& hammer in hand

climbed past the steel-gated
screen door
looked at the shorty w/a gleaming
scalp

shining bright
blk girl lips smack at the sight of jesus
everybody 'round these parts bend corners quick

so she like where you been?

she question his arrival
late as a summer sunset but still hot
& on time

praise be
jesus don't hold grudges
come right into the crib
blk girl staring w/salty eyes
       as flyy as he made her

& he like:
that's good

REDBONE DANCES

If you ain't never watched your parents kiss
          ain't never had them teach you
'bout the way lips will   bend & curve
against a lover's affirmation

If you ain't watched the knowing nod
of sweethearts worn away & soft
as a speaker box's blown out hiss

If you ain't sure there was a time when
their eyes held each other like a nexus
breaking the lock to dip dark marbles
into hopeful corners of a shot glass

If you ain't never known a Saturday night
slick with glittered promises & clouds
wrapped wet   in a Pendergrass croon

If you ain't been taught how
a man hold you close *so close*
. . . it look like a crawl

If you ain't had the memory
of your mother & father sliding
hip to hip   Their feet whisper
a slow shuffle & shift   Her hand

on his neck   grip the shoulder of
a man that will pass his daughters
bad tempers   & hands like bowls

If you ain't watched a man
lean into a woman His eyes
slide across her bronze
            His hands
pillared in her auburn hair   Her
throat   holds   the urge
to hear how her voice sounds against
the wind of him

If your skin can't fathom the fever
of something necessary as this

Then you can't know the hurricane
of two bodies   how   the bodies
can create the prospect of a sunrise
how that sunrise got a name
            it sound like: a blues song;
a woman's   heart *breaking;*

From the record player   skipping
            the sky   almost
blue

JAUNDICE

You came differently thrashing your limbs until the blood
    spilled clean
Sun ain't even set before Bam claimed "she got my smile"—I
    thought he said "spine"
A disaster always got a woman's name attached to its arrival
You come just howling—a yellow baby born too soon

The sun ain't even set before Bam claimed "she got my smile"—I
    thought he said "spine"
They say this is how the walls sweat with sin when a woman
    speaks
You come justa howlin'—a yellow baby born too soon
When you squealed a welcome song I knew you'd be thunder in
    my throat

They say this is how the walls sweat with sin when a woman
    speaks
Say her mouth is her greatest weapon & her tongue be a grenade
    pin unclipped
When you squealed a welcome song I knew you'd be thunder in
    my throat
Knew I'd stretch sound across an Oakland intersection to save
    your adorn & tick

Say her mouth is her greatest weapon & her tongue be a grenade
    pin unclipped

Bam was a thief. He stole my sunshine when I threatened to
change the locks on my heart
Knew I'd stretch sound across an Oakland intersection to save
your adorn & tick
Eclipsed your smile under the safest parts of Oklahoma &
promised to kill you before Spring

Bam was a thief. He stole my sunshine when I threatened to
change the locks on my heart
I got tired of his hands hoarding my memories. He got tired of
my weapon getting in the way
Eclipsed your smile under the safest parts of Oklahoma &
promised to kill you before Spring
You twister toxemia child—I knew you would be the birth of a
different me

I got tired of his hands stealing my memories. He got tired of
my weapon getting in the way
You came differently thrashing your limbs until the blood
spilled clean
You twister toxemia child—I knew you would be the birth of a
different me
A disaster always got a woman's name attached to its entrance

REAL FRIENDS

so A'toya wanna fight
you   her ass big
as every mama you done
met   & you only want
to be her friend   only
want to stop folks from
laughin'   she
wear clothes from the
plus-sized store so
she ain't got the GUESS
patch   on   her jeans
& her   jheri curl is long
          but you   think
you can show her how real
friends stick around &
don't let folks laugh &
she say   we best
friends today   but
tomorrow   she goin'
find her a new friend
you can see it in her eyes
cause she shift them so
much   you can't
ever tell what she really
thinking

REDBONE ON FIGHTING

When she come to grab
you, pick up a garbage
can & work that big ass girl.

Swing on her like you did
your brother when he
ripped your favorite book.

Don't cry—swing! Hell
I already knew she was trouble ...
Don't nobody with good sense
forget to close the screen door.

CUL DE SAC FOLKLORE

a cul de sac can bury the mouths of its young
rinse their dreams in pot liquor
call it heart disease
blood pressure   a rising star   & the babies
want to belong to something real   the
american dream sold as fashionable folklore
mama work hours 'til the cul de sac becomes
father figure   the blood of its children
a pulsating wound beneath   each hand
latched tight against the mouth of prey

REDBONE PLAYS BONES

she got a mean side-eye
got a mean hand too

you can tell   how she   hold
the dominoes   she been here

here: the head of the table
the driver in the passenger seat

first   to unlock   the chain in the
morning first to admit she mourns

almost everything   except   this
type of hand-on-hand combat

she tell you "dig in the graveyard"
she slur her cognac   she laugh

arched   eyebrow   smoke churns
across her face   cloaks   her restlessness

in folds of grey she asks "who you laughing at?"
in an almost serious tone   no one answers her

cause   she   got questions for
everything *like* it ain't her first time

hearing her own voice echo
"all the time" she say "she ain't got"

before tapping her wrist   she rise
into a stumble step from the table

and swing like a rag down the hall
close her door and lock it slow

a curious child jumps to   fill the empty
seat   eager to know how the graveyard

got so full. little nosy pretends   such small fingers
can count losses   as quickly as   Redbone did

slam the table   triumphantly, puncture
the air with "DOMINO!"   before

knocking over the ashtray and her abandoned
cigarette burning down to the   filter   slow

you ain't never been the type
to let a man climb his ocean
of a body through your bedroom
window   not like Li Li
she   first-born daughter
to a correctional baton
she learn quick   how to sweet talk
a man away from his sensibilities
           & you be: the type
of swoon & shadow frame
& sickle moon   sliced into the
mimic of your best friend
     you point your toes
into the canvas of your bleached
Keds   straighten your stretch pants
in plain sight   &   wait
for any boy's heat   to greet
your famished eyes   burnt orangish brown
under the delirious   sun
           Li Li always called you
pretty   always   called   the next
morning when Steven   slink
his body from her bed   or her
      window   ajar
ya'll laugh   the rotary phone
a coil of secrets tapping against

the carpeted floor   she
sigh   a breath of fresh crisp

moving dangerous against   your virgin ears

it feel like something inside is on fire

You sneak Clifton into the house & wait
    quietly behind the locked door
for the heavens to open up & lick you clean off the earth.
When that ain't happen you give him your hand & walk him
to your room. You stand opposite against the wall & talk slow.
    Easy breaths.
The summer leaves a sunburn everywhere except in your
    mouth.
It isn't as romantic as you imagined.   You pull away & feel
like you got caught stealing.

REDBONE & BOX WINE

You were the hardest to raise—
you just needed too much. By
the time you was thirteen maybe
fourteen years old, I was done
being anybody's Mama. I had
us a nice place, a desk job for the
State, I had me some friends with
no drama. Just music & Kools
Playing cards & box wine. You like
to drive me crazy always asking
'bout Bam, where & when he
coming to visit . . . If he goin' send
more of them earrings in the broken
china box that turn ya ears all types
of nasty colors. I still don't know
where they came from—all I know
is I smell another woman on the
hot plastic . . . But hell, I let you be.
You ain't got much to remember him
by nohow. You got his eyes though,
. . . Yeah, them all his.

BL_ _K GIRL

God/Who dat?
—*Alice Walker*

cause you ain't seen none of them praying/when
they crack/baby skull/open wide/on the side-
walk/call it jump in/like a Black child need to
know / how destructive a leap can be / like his
black skin know what "in" mean/in the first
damn place/they say family and gang / all the same
so it ain't mean nothing different/
when your uncle/ sit over you/ let his fist/ get to
dancin' on your Black girl head/   &   your Bl__k
girl nose/&   your   Blk girl chin/be   all
mangled/like a disaster   tailored just for your
frame/ & he think he testin' you/for the waters/
so the sharks know/you the toughest meat/   &
that's the shit that will save a bitch/so   you take
each blow/like a puppy   drunk   on its own
whimper/   hold his three-year-old daughter/
as far   a w a y as possible/ his scabbed knuckles
                    swinging wildly against the dusk of a girl

CUTLASS

there is a gun / silver / rusted / cutlass 2 door sedan / grey hoody: you.
there is a gun / rust / the color of forever / your play-brother
got a lead foot

PLAY BROTHER

play-brother swing the corner / like you already pop / silver

REDBONE WINS ROUND 1

she twisted the bottle cap
like she wish she could twist
his neck   & the argument
reaches across his gnarled soft demeanor

his cheek—the only touchable
thing she can find these days
her hands—drape across her own face,
      instinctively & quick,
so so so quick—even still
he quicker he thunder c l a p s
the cheekbone   the temple
the lips   bruises her
into a rainbow woman
      stares   incredulously—
wonders how she held the glass
bottle so still—how his thunder ain't
drop her swift into slump
—where she found the nerve

she listens to these questions
coiling themselves around the
room   drops her hands to her side
      a renewed defiance stretching
itself into the length of the kitchen
wall   she hears the silence

a mission bell   a *clang* alarming
the impending storm   she sets   the
bottle upright on the counter   ignores
the rapid tempo in her skull   hushes
away her tears   speculates
this will end soon.

BEST TIME III

the best time we had as a teenager
was the last time we saw Deon alive
sideline smack-talker with unwelcoming eyes
boa constrictor of a boy
he took a girl's stuff even after she pushed him away
she tells us the story in the locker room
other girls earshot near
the newspaper bleeds his obituary
all our girl bodies hold up the steam crusted walls
me too escapes a whimper from the echoing
the room now cold enough to clink our teeth

when you are a deep amber & your jheri curl is a distant memory
& your shape is swollen in the perfect places & the boys remember
your name & your first and last crush sings to you come here with
a lilt in his walk & his pale tongue coaxes you towards him & you
smile because you remember the sun wrinkles your darkness so you
pull corners of your bright face & squint like you practiced in the
bathroom mirror where only a hint of your gap-tooth smile lingers
like a wager & you think of the time you danced in the basement
with the brown boy in a half-moon fade   even then you were
frowning in the dark trying to figure out if his fingers should shove
themselves between your cotton & denim like that because you
could not understand the wet & you frowned & he stopped & you
thought i want to but his eyes were all over your face & his smell was
copper & so close & you sighed & he stopped & in the dark he says
come here & he is what you've always wanted & it is in the senior
class lock-in which is a storm of hormones endo smoke & everclear
& everyone is touching someone & no one is frowning including
you & it's like the time when stories are passed during homeroom
& locker rooms & you always wanted to have a story for the cold
tiles when there are only bra straps & lip gloss & hair brushes &
(smiles where no frowns are found because) you don't know what it
is like to lose yourself in a shadow you only know how to fold each
breath like a Blk girl mistake into the borrowed white*stretch* jeans
pocket   &   wait

BEST TIME VI

you ain't had freedom
'til you climb on bus 62
& head to the closest mall
for a good seat at the girl fight

no one could tell us
hella ain't a word
we say it like a comma
we say it to keep the sadness slow

before them girls jumped the new blue from up north
four girls stood on top of her limp body
the cobalt top torn from her impeccable frame
the frozen yogurt shop buzzing
w/a gang of girls in red tops
& hella bloody shoes

VAST.

you held Justin's hand in the dark
in the garage corner while everyone
else pretended to not watch

you both were slippery tongues
& new with the idea of girlfriend
& drunk off the parentless gaze
of a house party

you held your breath & his hand wandered
he tripped across your skin
his eyes brown & one lazy

remain partially closed & full
aware of the dark
his lap a hot brick

& your desire to be wanted
a cooling dam   so
vast   it drenched you both

ACID

i want to tell you a story it goes like this/your stomach is already hot w/giggles cause you ain't never heard somebody worth something to listen to say the word "slut" like this/& i guess you right/but the story still needs to be told bout the new girl from los angeles/& the time she moved into your neighborhood/her first week smelled like a sweet valley high chapter except she is nothing like Jessica/no blue-green eyes/no blonde hair/nothing except her girl shape & her dangerous eyes & she is everything like you   except the boys like her & not when no one is looking   & everyday everyone is looking/her acid washed jeans announce she is not from here/she is different   you think you could want to be this type of different/you think you could want this type of different holding your name/after school everyone walks home by the swallow of oak trees/near the quiet bend & soccer post furthest from the park & you want to follow the crowd to sit beneath the shade but you have chores/but you have not been remembered yet/& acid washed jeans girl is not your friend/yet/so you have no real reason to pretend you belong & the next day you try not to be impressed/your mouth a silent O when you return to school/the new girl w/acid washed jeans is no longer shiny/no longer new/just another brown girl/gone blk/& unwanted/& almost closer to you & her name is a bone in their mouths/all cause her acid washed jeans were caught around her ankles at the park w/one of the loudest of swaggers/he claims the prize/he raise his hands/he say w/a barrage of snarls "she stink"

"she nasty" "she let me . . ." & after school no one is walking
w/her no one is following her unless to laugh at her call her
"fishgirl" call her anything but her name

BEST TIME X

before anyone can say you talk too loud
you turn up your volume for good measure
by now you've learned to protect yourself
by now you've perfected the art of swinging
    a girl by her hair
    the grip of your fist
    when you wrench at her head
    & twist her jaw like a barbie doll
ain't no one safe

                not after someone left Tameka half burned
                   & buried in a valley ditch

TRIVIA

what is a bullet?

> *what dies when no matter whom it loves wrongly*

what is a bullet?!

> *what is a hollowing instrument. what else is there?*

what is a bullet??

> *what is a certain gone.*
> *a collapsing; or even an implosion/ if you're lucky.*

what is a bullet!?

> *what is luck to a Black body.(?)*

what is a bullet . . . ?

> *what is a new & improved lynching.*

THE HEIST

On St. John's and Franklin Avenue
there is a bullet hole in the pay phone.
He reaches out to touch its opening
and I am instantly jealous. He tells
the story about the robbery and the
bodega as the CCTV follows our journey.
The new neighbors stumble drunk
from a new and overpriced pub,
its décor a hodgepodge of old tile and
rusted picture frames. Even on the sidewalk
we feel out of place. We control the volume
in our tone. We jerk at the megaphone
symphony slurred by the white girl
in torn jeans. She is on stage. She is
a Rockstar. This corner of crime and
dirt and fix and curry is her audience.
She knows she owns the sidewalk. She
wants another beer, her boyfriend's lips,
the world's attention. Her pout says this
has been promised to her since birth. Her
friends shake their head at us apologetically.
We nod. Accept this favor with disgust and
envy. We walk away. Further down the block.
He no longer remembers the story about the
bodega. Or the robbery. It is too silent. He
walks on my right, near the curb, to keep

me safe. My hand wants to brush his—but
this is Brooklyn. It is late and that's just something
people don't do.

1981

The first time person you attempt to test the well of love you can hold for a girl it will come clothed like your kin   a sister who will make you pay   sister will wiggle her finger   like a secret   & you love her so much you can't stand to not know what makes her so smart to your adoring eyes   sometimes you pretend you are her & wear her PJs   the ones with the yellow rainbows across the chest   the ones she leaves tossed at the edge of the daybed every time she retreats to her father's house   & you don't go over there as much cause your mama say NO   & she let you cry or sometimes   they just wait   'til you sleep before they creep down the driveway   or sometimes   you forget to cry   until they walk back up the driveway the next day   & you got a name for what pain   slams in your chest   but brother & sister   both older mama-look-alikes   climb across the pavement drop their bags   & return to you   on the lawn   you wait   & your sister know you love her cause you do whatever she demands   & she wiggle her finger   she   got a secret   &   your brown*brown* eyes open wide w/huh?   the water hose an unsteady dam in your hands shoot the dirt up from the grass   & spray dark droplets on your face   but you can't be bothered   so you scurry across the wet lawn close enough to hear her whisper "mom found you in the gutter & we told her to give you away but she ain't listen."

1992

The sun was always hot in the valley & you still ain't know why
your best friend stopped answering your calls   until your older
sister walk into the house   her smile   a   blinding sun
          she ain't never been nice   not since she tried to drown
          you in Mrs. Gloria's backyard pool back when you was
          only 6 years old &   Blk & bony   & she was 11 &   not
          so   boney
          but she Black   & she remind you *we ain't got the same*
          daddy   but you ain't care none
          that ain't how your family built   then she stomps *don't*
          call my daddy your daddy
          so you don't say a word   not until she out the room
cause he say   *call me whatever you want*   & he nice   & he
here   & she overhear you too   & her eyes slit into   a
Bl___k you ain't never seen before but you don't care   cause
now   you   got   TWO daddies   & this kind of math make
you smile   cause you got somebody that want you
          you giggle a little   & she got a surprise
          she say   & the pool was so blue
& you just learned how to swim   you want her to be proud   but
you   got   a   daddy   in   jail   so   sometimes   you   try   too
hard   you say   *what?*   & she say wait a minute so she can swim
closer   & she smiling like   she the sun   like you & her is
more than friends   but real blood sisters   & you wait for her
to get to your side of the pool before she reach her hand way up

& you watch her fingers spread against the light   & she
she bring her arm down so hard
you can't believe the sound   it's like a c r a c k   like a
bat   like you only see blk
     & the blue is blk now too & her smile is big   until
something move her hand away from your sunken face   but
this is a gone gone memory & now you sit in the living room &
you ain't swam in Mrs. Gloria's pool since she died   & your big
sister still the sun   just more angry   so when she sashay thru
the house like a shark in turquiose water   you know what her
kind of smile mean   & you still a little bit scared   even if you
bigger than her   cause   her eyes are slits of blk   again
so you scoot away from her   away from the door   away
from her outstretched hand
     & you scared to look too close   to the hand   instead
your   eyes   tighten   &   you   squeak   *what?*   &   she
say   HERE!   before she toss a keychain at you   it's a
plastic one w/a picture on its insides & you no longer worried
about her hands   or her smile   you too blinded   by
the photograph: your only sister & your former best friend
horseback riding & grinning at the camera lens   your blood a
big hot   &   all them unanswered calls ringing in your head

CUL DE SAC PLOT

a cul de sac ain't nothing but a row
generational trauma   an heirloom mausoleum
belts wrapped around knuckles
hot wheel tracks mimic skin reaper

each box a secret mirror plantation memoirs
ain't nothing dead 'til it got its hands & feet cut off

even then
it don't die right away

THE RINK

the skating rink
is the best place
to fall in

splinter proof
floors
walls with cushions

the body
is most forgiving
here

the couples skate
hip to hip
side to side
footwork intimate as a kiss
red and orange
toe stoppers
accent the tongues
flying songs
a soundjoy

the backwards spin
the forwards sprawl
the beginning of a turn
backspin

turn
break
turn
a cheap and torn backdrop
red cushions padded wall
the floor full of skid marks

can turn
the flesh
the tangled mess

can remind
through laughter
& tethered joy

the body
is most forgiving
here

BETTY SEZ

Betty didn't take kindly to a man's
instruction. She preferred to tell him
where to shove his opinion instead

my grandaunt was the oldest to a
brother with bricks for hands. Her glare
promised a gunbutt'n for any man that
touched her expensive handbag.

At the age of 90, she didn't hesitate to swing,
cutting the wind in half with her sinewy arms.
She snarled, *he trynna steal my stuff.*

She was usually right.

Betty Sez

she taught her sister-in-law three things:

1. how to cock a gun
2. how to bet on racehorses & win
3. how to run / why to run / & when to stand tall against a
   dynamite suit of a man,
   a cigarette stiff on the cliff between her lips the entire time.

Betty Sez

I got a secret:

I knew I would be nobody's bride

It's better like 'dis

                    Besides . . . I ain't into taking gifts
                    from horses
                    no way.

CHURCH HEAT

Grandma Coco's church is uppity
Everyone sings like a bad opera
More white people than black folks

Not enough Black folk here
A neatly braided brown girl enters

The double doors close out the zephyr
The women in their choir robes, swaying with eyes closed

This is the reason Grandma Coco rise early on Sundays
The reason she bellow her tenor bell
The second place she prayed for Redbone
Only second
To the head of her wood dining room table

Grandma Coco love her church
Love her church friends & them boring sermons
Love to bring her grandbabies, a candle returned to their dull eyes
Love to see they dresses clean
& coarse curls pinned up on each side

She ain't notice how they slouch in they seats
How they dog-ear the new bibles
with cable knit tights corkscrewed at the ankles
Swallowing hemlines whole

ORANGE RINDS

Grandma told you the story orange rinds upturned on their backs beneath her fingertips/she grin & say she ain't care (much) about the sneaking around or the drugs or the (mishandling) money & you believe her cause she got the silky hair you always want & the brown skin that promise you goin' be cute to someone other than ya mama/one day but today your jheri curl is bubbling up a song on the back of your neck—a crisp onyx because the California sun is not as forgiving as your grandmother be & she peel each orange almost smile at the thought of your Grandpa Dempsey & everyone call him Dee like his name so sweet you just gotta get it off they tongue & he just one pretty skinned wavy haired slick firecracker spitshine of a man she s m i l e he the type to wink at a woman & watch her return with a chicken plate & two biscuits w/out ever acknowledging the wife attached to the ring on his left hand he the only husband quick enough to give Grandma two children before her mouth change the locks on the front door she suck the titian flesh "any man forget his god long enough to call you a Blk bitch be the first man to get gone"

SPINDLE GREASE

she learned to perch
like her mama
over the stove
frying some good cut
of fish in a pot of lard
popping
her hip like Friday sang
her favorite tune

she learned to pose
each hand on her hips
to make sure ya back
—bone don't slip
like her mama
said it might
& the hopscotch
chant promised

she learn to arch
her bridge
her tower
her spindle
her teeth

suck ready
like her mama be
every Friday night
her daddy sleep
in front the tv

Bam got tight eyes
    Real tight
He crazy, girl
    But fun to be around
He so funny
    He jokester & party starter
He the oldest of them boys over on Alcatraz
    He love them birds—the pigeons
That's what I heard
    He got a cage in the backyard
He got a cage on the roof
    He make the cage out of cardboard & wire
He scale roofs
    He think he (can) fly
I heard he stole the pigeon from Albert's coop
    & when all them boys went looking for Bam
He just waited for they ass on the stoop
    I heard they went looking through his flock
Heard they ain't found nothing
    Heard they still ain't believe him
Hell, I heard his daddy made him fight 'em one-on-one
    Everybody know they call him Bam cause of his hands
His eyes so tight & you never know when he go boom!
    He always had quick hands
That's how he call them birds back home
    The rough of his calloused hands clapping & singing loud

That's how he fought them boys
> His hands ain't but a blur
He slap against the wind & win
> Them boys ain't never forgot
But hell, what they goin' do—he see everything
> His eyes so tight you never know what he thinking
He crack his knuckles & they jump on him
> He clap his hands fast & it sound like matchwood
They say "it" sound like firecrackers
> He say the birds can hear him that way
He say if he clap loud enough they know to come home
> He say home with his mouth big & smiling
But his eyes never change, he so handsome
> They say that's how he knew where to hide Albert's pigeon
Say he hid Albert's bird behind the homemade cage's broken board
> His eyes shine like crazy laughter man lightning
He got hands like his daddy
> His hands so quick
> > —They steal anything worth something

the blkest night
be a Blk girl w/a trench for s k i n
smell like a man
she ain't never
goin' have/no ring
to call home/no/way

When I think of my grandfather:

I never think of him as a fighter.
I think of him military memory
hand tools, slapping five & sipping coffee

a chipped cup to his lips. Easy. Like his
smile. Like a man that loved the Blues.

I never think fist / shove / pummel
loosening teeth or bursting lips like fruit.
I only remember a kind man.

Beckoning me to the kitchen table, his legs

crossed noose-like in a pair of paint-speckled
jeans. His smile, a ray of whatever brightens

the sun. He always offered me a sip of his coffee.

Sweet & mud dark.

static turns the TV screen into a grey overcast of noise/& the stars know this kind of swoon/ how the tension of a tongue don't mean much/to a black sky//when i hold his hand to my chest/ i think/ he believes — i am the sky// so i say: i am the sky & everything around me is smoke stained // the subway train is running right now/ a lover is returning home late but still // nobody will sleep in the lover's house/until the key kisses the lock hello/ & followed by the noisy silence of a refrigerator hum/ or a library book turning beneath the glowing husk// this is how most hearts sing murmur// this is why my heart whispers run// & the moon wishes someone would wait for her to return to the apartment/ & the moon is gracious & giving & who will hold her when she nods herself almost awake/ exhausted & dilapidated across town/into a too small pre-war apartment/ & the moon cannot remember when there was a warm palm to wipe away her tired/////////////// the way she wipes away the sun's bruised setting/ every night the way the moon give her shoulders to the light last night, the moon crooned/ i've been running from the freedom of my own blood/ i know lonely . . . i know . . . i know . . . i know . . . / because be/////////////////////////////

she done
gone lost her mind
gone black blank
rubble rubbish
piles and piles
of smoke
      clear caved in chest
      spread beds burn
          before ashes spread
             down 95 South
in a land of Mary
in a land of black and merry
in a land
      where Redbone found
      clouds to
      corner her
      like he did—
        once
she fled for her baby and her *baby's* baby
she think smoke can't find them there
too // like she can't see the clouds thick with
almost   when it spread   way up North
UP near the boulevard   where a planet
cradles the biggest stones for home   here
her baby   and her *baby's* baby find a lullaby
in the belly of a steel horse Redbone hungry for hustle

gristle crack break   *baby's* jaw run slack   her child
boomerang dey mama's sunshine to a southern city
with a cardinal's nest for a name Redbone   find smoke there
too//   smoke less grey   almost white
so white   she dream   clouds   again
          dream   arms full of her *baby's*   baby
          she is always a
fragment of a coast-sludged woman
          always a mother
heaving grief the size of her only name
          she be:
          missing her own mother
          swaddled in smoke and guilt

— it kills everything:
                    a people
                    a home
                    or a spirit — *yea*
guilt can kill a spirit
too

LACQUER

the woman will swallow her tongue
steal a spittle of secrets between the teeth
loosen her enamel with an untold thing
call it a cavity & bite down   hard

PITEOUSNESS

her lungs are closing
in   swallowing her
own name like a grief
torn lover   i am losing
the fight to remain neutral

RITA CROSS REDBONE

And then   there was   Rita;
a bullhorn of a woman   slick   wit Bam's
name in her mouth   from the entrance
of the corner store   sweet   sweat
sliding   down her chest   leaned
inside the glass casing   condensation
dragging its tongue across the gold and white
cans of cheap Bud Lite   Rita called Bam's name
          thick with spit   to remind everyone they be   fucking
Rita   a piss-colored   hip-heavy woman
a purple hickey sly smirking from her exposed
skin   and Redbone wasn't nothing
but another yella heffa   out to take her man
Rita laughed   her tongue   poked out   like a   child
she tapped her finger   against the taut skin of her
growing belly   held Bam's arm tight with the other
red fingernails   *pinchandrelease*   pinch   and
pinch again to make sure   he   was   real—and hers
like the last white teddy bear   from a street fair full
of dust   Bam   didn't look at her   not once
Rita shift her foot   and smile   tight

HIJACK

you thirst for no in the key of a loyal throat & he will teach you a
song you will hum for three decades thereafter
you will be hurt you will be hurt you will be hurt a ripple
until your 30th birthday until all you know is thirst until every
man is just a hi jack handshake waiting to happen beneath your
skirt & the night will smell like all the things no one cares about
like the night you almost stayed w/a cute smile w/beanstalks for
arms   how his hunger for your obedience will toss you into
a Manhattan scaffold: excited by the soundlessness of crushed
bone

BL_CK GIRL

> *I can't look in her eye, seeing all that lonely, and think*
> *I got a right to keep being me*
> *—Patricia Smith*

a Brooklyn studio   kitchen the size of your mama's
bathroom   the brownstone stone blessed by fried
chicken smolder & he's dressed in white   linen

your box braids   swing   a   single swagger   his
eyes dance destruction   a pair of four alarm fires alight
he spreads   each   flame   across your breasts   slick   your
name like his gin   you ignore his sun dusted date   &
she waits   like a mother told her women must do   &
you   just an Oakland intersection   signaling Brooklyn men
with your curious accent
because you don't just walk into nobody's house party
his smile   a question mark   his date's slender   haunts the night
air   & you brown dirty dark black blackest night midnight blue
Bl_ _k girl

without ever forgetting your name

Sometimes you ain't 'posed to love up on nobody
like that. Sometimes it's too hard on the bones and
no one but your own self know what you want to do
with the weight of it all—only you know what you
can't take. Everybody told me what to do when it came
to Bam.

My eyes still heavy from all the sleep I ain't got and
my back on fire from the baby trying to break free
through my spine. I tell 'em "No. We gone make this
family make sense." But what I want to say is "We gone
fall into the night like we fell into each other and it won't
hurt no more. 'Cause I hurt when we ain't together. I hurt
'cause it remind me of the my daddy, how he made my momma
cry, how her tears carried me to sleep on the nights I forgot
to close the door.

When we ain't together, I am reminded that I'm broken,
That my heart ain't got no locks 'cause it ain't got no doors
'Cause they took away my doors when I was only a baby—
Don't nobody wanna hear about a baby girl with a missing
door! That sound too much like blame. And I'm tired of how
my fingers bend and all I want is for some reason to stay
put. I want something that stay mine. My first husband
got a mean space between his chest. Took my first and second
born out of spite. He's a spiteful man. They grow in my

belly, burn my heart with pride, crush my smile into little
pieces when they cry—they was mines.
He was never mines.

My belly big with my only son was just a reason enough to cheat
the first time. So by the time I got me a man, who make me feel
like I got doors on my everything, like I got a key—like I
control the movement in my body—I ain't care too much
that he cheat too. My first husband got me used to a bed
smelling like thangs that wasn't mine. I got so used to it
by the time I met Bam I was happy someone wanted
to fight the devil for me. I was happy even if the only one he fought
was me. Every bruise every tremor match my hair and the gap in
my teeth and it keep him coming back. Telling me sweet
everything, I don't start the mess but I ain't running to the Valley
neither. Besides, he say he goin' fight the world for what's his.

You can't tell me that ain't love. You can tell me anything but
    that . . .

GREEN EARTH

Walt lived on the porch
At the end of Helen Street
His glass-eyed call out
To any ear that would catch it

Come see me tonight

Once, his invitation crept up slow
& sowed intentions across my nape
But Oakland raised a goon
Reared me with pit bulls and possums
Only snarl I know is

I'll cut you in pieces & feed you the meat

Elsie Jean ain't appreciate the candor
Walt, all glassy-eyed think my hands too neat
For the kill

Six months later, Walt sat on the porch
Of the house at the end of Helen Street
When it burned to the ground
No one heard him scream

We don't know who started the fire
My ears suspect his mouth
Begat the flame
All that alcohol
& all that godlessness
Spill sloppy be birthing ash

I ain't smile none
I ain't bound to bloom at a certain death
Still, I say to Elsie Jean

Ain't no frame fit to sit on a porch
or this green earth
for too long like that

ODE TO FEET

you ten can wink chancletas into silence
you almost a dozen, a dirty pleasure for Tony
& the red tiles of a nail salon in Brooklyn,
you coo, like no one's business

you left foot suspicious
alive w/stitches
kiss a seal across the skin

where the joints wheeze
because the ankle is jealous
& the surgery damaged each feeler
named after foods

the corn is still delicious

your lover will palm cocoa butter
against the base of the foot
a hoof
no, a canoe

here, a girl will want feet like her mother
instead, a girl will earn feet like her father

        or a slave
it's all the same
the digits
add up

LOVE SONG

For Elsie Jean & Pau

i never heard my grandmother
say "i love you" to my grandfather.
my grandfather would sooner say he
loved us ashy brown pawn pieces &
"children, your grandma just mean"
he'd smile with honesty weeping
from his wrinkles.
my grandmother, a brownstone dish

proper & hot water cornbread—
paid him no mind. her neck
a swivel swing. cracked his old man
banter, ignored him like
loud sirens serenading oakland
sky on friday.
      "i ain't stuttin' you"
she waved, kitchen spoon swim
in gravy or collard greens. her hips
swayed along to the rhythm under
her breath. his eyes danced along—
she pretended she know
he was checkin' for her beat.

later, the cancer ate through his
bones like chalk   she stay oiling
his flaking skin & scrubbing fluid from the walls
with clorox   she stay humming a song
through the nights   his lungs   lurched
for air   only her hips & his memory
 still knew the words.

The name of this poem is:
How to write a poem about Ferguson
Or

The name of this poem is:
How a black man dies and no one makes a sound
Or

The name of this poem is:
Everywhere is Ferguson
Or

The name of this poem is:
When the moonrise sounds like gunshots
Or

The name of this poem is:
How to teach your babies to walk and not run, ever
Or

The name of this poem is:
How to teach your babies to carry a wallet
the size of their smile
Or

The name of this poem is:
How to smile & not make yourself a target
Or

The name of this poem is:
How to write a poem the same size of Emmett Till's lungs
Or

The name of this poem is:
How to write a poem about America's thirst
Or

The name of this poem is:
Black blood'll keep you thirsty
Or

The name of this poem is:
I'm Still Thirsty: An American Horror Story
Or

The name of this poem is:
How to write an escape route from a tornado
Or

The name of this poem is:
How to write an escape route
when the tornado's name is Stop & Frisk
Or

The name of this poem is:
How walk the streets without fearing
someone will cut your neck open
Or

How to walk into a boardroom
without fearing someone will cut your legacy open
Or

How to walk without asking for it
Or

How to walk without asking for it
Or

How to determine what "asking for it" looks like
Or

The name of this poem is:
How "asking for it" feel like a church bombing
Or

The name of this poem is:
How to not intimidate nobody in 3 small steps
Or

The name of this poem is:
How to use your science books as Teflon
& how that still might not work
Or

The name of this poem is:
How to write about the one time you held a gun
Or

The name of this poem is:
How to write about the one time you had a gun pointed to your face
Or

The name of this poem is:
How write about the one time you had a gun pointed to your face
Or

The name of this poem is:
How write about the one time you had a gun pointed to your face
Or

The name of this poem is:

How write about the one time you had a gun pointed to your
    face

Or

The name of this poem is:

How to write a poem from the perspective

of a cop's gun

< >

a cop's Taser

< >

a cop's baton

< >

a cop's boot

Or

The name of this poem is:

How to write poem without r e p e a t i n g yourself

Or

The name of this poem is: "it ain't got no name"

The name of this poem is series of numbers

The numbers sing fear at night & warn me sweetly

You should be afraid to have a son

BECAUSE . . .

After & for Patricia Smith

Because you were born a crumbling mountain
Because they made a song in God's throat
Called it   Motown   Called it   Black woman
Called it   "what cannot be killed"

Because babies call you *mama mammy nanny*
Because the black on your skin sings a lemon bath siren
Because no one asks if it hurts to be this Black
Because no one asks if it hurts to be this kind of woman
Because woman and Black mean silent   mean invisible
Because you goin' fight for her babies before your own
Because you know they goin' kill your babies

Because Kadiatou Diallo
Because Sybrina Fulton
Because Valerie Bell
Because a Black mother know ain't no ocean big enough to
    carry away the corpses

Because you moan
Because you howl
Because you howl
Because you howllll   llllll   llllll   llllll

Because you know the belly croon a ravenous song
Because the sound call the babies back home

Because you home
Because you home
H o m e you be
          Cause you sleep w/your hands thrashing
A lemon wedge beneath the bed frame to keep away an
    orchestra of ghosts

Because Kadiatou Diallo
Because Sybrina Fulton
Because Valerie Bell
Because Mamie Till
Because your Black mother's heart be home to a sleepless ocean
& even the moon shut its mouth *tight*   to listen

A)   father gifts you his hands 2) your
mother laughs w/the breath of a ghost C)
no one remembers how much you cried
5) there are more houses in your throat
than one can count E) you forgot how to
count because you forget how to say i love
you 8) your grandmother is a steeple 9)
you love how love sounds more than you
know how it works 10) you love how love
works more than you know how to hold
the pieces 11) your father showed you how
love works with his absent mouth J) i love
you K) your grandmother is a steeple—you
are only a cemetery meandering 14) you
can bury anything inside these hands 14.5)
you are best w/dirt 15) you wear a printed
t-shirt to the local farmer's market—the
blk letters read: do not get lost here, there
is nothing left but white soot

IF LOVE IS FOR THE FISHES

i breathe them in each night
a shallow breath of scaly skin
i breathe deep & think
of the shrimp's crooked smile
i breathe deeper & am thankful
for the lobster's claw
i know this is a type of love
and dream for their flesh to never know harm nor hurt
to never know run and hide

i know this is a type of love
because my cheeks grow warm
      my hands fling at the stars
      i dance a dance all my own
      there is music in my chest

i know this is a kind of love
because i think of my family
how they smile & i smile too
i always think of love & soft feather beds
the water is perfect for here & when i close
my eyes i only see a garden growing upwards
towards the sun that is really a smile
& the water washes away the dust
of my night screams
love is an open door

a boat swimming against a purple glory
& syrup spun sugar
& i breathe & breathe & breathe
love 'til we become

PICKPOCKET

at night, his maw opens wide
my name sings out like a broken swan
each syllable a fluttering mess of "yes"
     a ligament torn testimony
     how I renamed myself
     singed my black into a shiny weapon
when I am in full arch, I be smoke
I be full lipped & moon woman
until sharp blues become slow "oh!"
watch my hands pickpocket the night
& bless everything I touch
until holy

PAST BEFORE

Ain't no man ya DADDY
     Sleep w/a broken bulb above the porch
     look carefully for the osseous phantom
     listen as it shuffles across threshold
a blue & gluttonous rat
Ain't NO man ya daddy
     Find a man w/soft eyes   Find a man
     w/no hands   Find a man w/no home
       PRAY
Ain't no MAN ya daddy
       When the first moon spills open like
a cavernous beast   & your mother
forgets to draw the curtains
of her smile
     the floorboards can   be the sledge hammer
     flush a splinter
     from the base
     beneath your big toe
     hold it like a pitchfork (or a gun)
        swing   (aim)
              crack

When growing up
the world is only
as big as your thumb

Only a sun or moon
can quake our atlas eyes
stumble into stillness
mouth of friction,
unfortunate & lovely accident
until now, or maybe,   before

My mother
bricked in me a firestack smokecloud
ring less Chaka Khan white/coked
& glorious
top turned out of control
swallow-sized fury birthed flaunt
black dusk stumbling tornado
                    counterclockwise sparrow

A woman can kill the small shackled cuckoo
a woman can sink with swim want
only a sky of an ocean can tread songs below
only the sinking can leave a stony brimstone brittle
with neglect

Reflective adhesive locked glare with gravel fists
mountains of godless designs
spectacle, hazy barbed against the whitest sheet/music

Full of breath
she is   bird swarm brilliant
a worn path to a wire-linked heart

An exact casualty intrigued muscle and scorch
Renaissance of the homeless hues
I want to color my age   grit perfect

Watch them leave the chalice dry

BEFORE, A PALINDROME

Before   I knew the ceramic-splintered man with copper fists
            I met a man w/my eyes placed strategically on his face

               the eve of my graduation the man
               with my grandpa's name found me
               my ultra perm bounced like an abandoned cord
               against my shoulders
               my smile followed

               he introduced me to his new wife
               a cathedral of lost things
               his step-daughter called him daddy with milk teeth
               after the memorable meeting
               he asked me for a ride to the ruptured nest of his
               mistress

               he called my hopscotch'd boyfriend *square*
               he called his cathedral a bitch
               I clenched the crater to the tender part of my mouth
               & he reeled back from my juggling switchblades
               he fell on the detonator & cried crack

               crack & crack & crack   &
               assault with a deadly weapon
               breaking and entering fortified his bones
               Pelican Bay transfers became home

West Oakland fame claimed his myth
He wanted a son to carry his paragon of patriarchy
The first grandbaby was a girl with his eyes placed
strategically on her face

He stole double-winged pigeons
a fluttering prayer
He had a coop
a mangled nest of barbed blood
He watched his mama and daddy fight
a flurry of wolves
He sat on the hood of a city car & dreamed of
country dew
He was the first-born dust cloud
to a pair of Louisiana pit stops
His parents stole themselves one night
tucked him tightly in the womb

Before   His parents stole themselves one night
tucked him tightly in the womb
He was the first-born dust cloud
to a pair of Louisiana pit stops
He sat on the hood of a city car & dreamed of
country dew

He watched his mama and daddy fight
a flurry of wolves
He had a coop
a mangled nest of barbed blood
He stole double-winged pigeons
a fluttering prayer

The first grandbaby was a girl with his eyes placed
strategically on her face

He wanted a son to carry his paragon of patriarchy
West Oakland fame claimed his myth
Pelican Bay transfers became home

breaking and entering fortified his bones
assault with a deadly weapon
crack & crack & crack   &

he fell on the detonator & cried crack
he reeled back from my juggling switchblades
I clenched the crater to the tender part of my mouth
he called his cathedral a bitch
he called my hopscotch'd boyfriend *square*

he asked me for a car ride to his mistress' ruptured
nest

his step-daughter called him daddy with rotten milk
teeth
after the memorable meeting
he introduced me to his new wife
a cathedral of lost things

my smile followed
my ultra perm bounced abandoned against my
shoulders
the eve of my graduation the man with my grandpa's
name found me

I met a man with my tight eyes placed strategically
on his face
I knew the ceramic-splintered man with copper fists

Before

GUN SHY

the gun is a school of fish
the gun is a house under water
the gun beats all the boys in tag
the gun answers the door before
anyone ever knocks

BLKEST NIGHT IS A BLK GIRL

the blk(est) night is a Blk
girl s w o l l e n smirk she
swell sideways saunter
a skillful solemn sound
in skimming sunsets the
key of lonely   ever since

Daddy high on drugs
He fresh outta jail for the first time
     in a long time.
He sits on the porch
     of the abandoned house on the corner of Adeline
     & let the sun bake him red.
Eldest daughter stomp around the corner
7-month-old seed on her hip & smiling
     always smiling
Daddy too high
     sky high his eyes
     to see his first homecoming
     going
Daddy too too gone
     his shirt a different color than its original print
     sullied in the soil of an Oakland underpass
Daddy too too gone
     his hair, black with white streaks
     slicked down with water and sweat.
Daddy too too gone
     his eyes only beads of black & anxious
Eldest daughter ain't never known this shaky tweak of a mortal
His shoulders twitched as she held out her only child
Her fear of him dropping another responsibility
     the breath lodged in her windpipe
Still Eldest hand over her only joy

Snapped the camera lens twice with a quickness
Snatched back her breath & baby before descending the stairs

Daddy ain't drop the baby
Daddy ain't drop the baby none
Daddy ain't never see the baby again
                      neither

REDBONE & AL GREEN

Love & Happiness
on vinyl just sound better.

Listen to this song . . .
Al sound like he miss
his Lady bad, don't he?

Listen.

I can't stand to hum along
to a man with a hole in his heart.

Rita moved into the Big House on Alcatraz and winked like a fox
in a chicken coop at the fading mirage of Redbone. Rita patted her
belly, smiled at his Bam's mother, cooed at his Bam's father like a blues juke
joint brewed in her blood. She sat on the stoop of Alcatraz, the
biggest house painted ultramarine sitting spread eagle in the middle
of Berkeley's intersection. The Big House was named after another
penitentiary reckless enough to have its own island. Rita sat on the
sprawling white teeth of the stairs and dreamed. She dreamed there
was no color red—no more Bam and Rita. No babies. She dreamed she
was always pregnant. She dreamt of empty hands. Behind her closed eyes
walls caved in and curved out, a waves of babies flushed themselves
in reverse from her past mistakes and into her patient arms. Her breasts
swelled warm with the idea. The heat unfolded in her chest dashed quickly
across her sternum before spreading dense through her belly. The fire
rumbled through her body causing a wretched tear to shoot from her
throat. She lay her head, heavy and spinning, on the white wood and
felt the hot rush, like the Oakland Hills brushfire, dance around her
belly and settle calmly in her lap. Her eyes flickered. She could only see
the babies, all of the tight-eyed babies surrounding her feet—she was
too busy dreaming to notice all the blood.

First Husband walk in
Let the light vanish
Whole room close like fist
Squeeze air from throat
Redbone legs shake
But Redbone eyes ain't move
Redbone whisper
"I make him stone. I make him stone."
Her eyes go crypt
Redbone's First Husband ain't but a man to Medusa
Redbone don't move
Don't give him reason to take first and second born
again
Redbone & First Husband watch children fiddle
With empty space of the apartment
Redbone watch First Husband stalk around room
First Husband dust every corner with cobalt eyes
Redbone chant in her head "I make him stone He can't hurt me,
I make him stone I make him stone I make him . . ."
Redbone heart turn trampoline
Redbone heart ain't never beat for First Husband
Like this
Redbone think "Love funny that way"
Redbone smirk "I do not love him, I make him stone, I have
    never

loved him like this, I make him stone, I make him stone, I make
   him . . ."
First Husband frown like he can hear what Redbone thinking
First Husband walk to front door & growl
"I'll be back Sunday"
Redbone palm swat door close
"I make him stone, I make him stone, I make him"

It broke my heart, when they moved Rita
in that house. The house where I snapped
peas with his mama and his sister. My
skin just itch thinking 'bout Rita and her
big ole hips up in there like she kin. Like
she family. She steady say she pregnant.
Just'a twisting her neck every time I come
'round Alcatraz. Like she own the porch or
something, like a yella girl need be afraid
of her 'bama-ass glare. That's why I tell him,
"you betta go get your girl" he say "you IS
my girl" I say "naw, ya' **girl** is in ya mama
house snapping peas!" He smile big, so big
his eyes close and grab my arm real tight
—like he can't let go even if he wanted to.
And I pretend I can't stand him when really
I just can't breathe. He too close. I can smell
the sun on his brown skin and I get jealous.
So I snatch away from him like my arm on
fire and start with the excuses "I got to work"
or "I got to meet my cousin" or "I'm 'bout to
go see my ex-husband" and Oooh! He hate
that last one. His eyes dance at me sharp
shooters like he wronged or something! Like
I'm the one with a woman claiming my first
born. His eyes go real dark and flare like

a burning bush. My arm still hot from his
touch. And he on me. His skin touching mine.
His arms everywhere and I won't let go. I try
to think of anything But his eyes, his hands . . .
I try to stop loving him. Tried to stop thinking
'bout his smile and how he smile bright as
the blackest sky. How he in my dreams just
running round causing me grief, giving me
indigestion, making me lose sleep. Thinking
'bout Bam keep my toes curling all on they own
when he call me "Red" and slur "girl" like he
hiding a Mississippi sharecropper in his throat.
He say my name like it's his favorite word like
a man in love with the way I sound on his tongue,
for a minute I forget all of it. I forget about Rita
and the son she done promised him, the kitchen
table with the matching white chairs and them
snapping peas—I swear I can only feel the earth
moving underneath us. Even after I climb into
the car and roll the window all the way down,
my arm stinging bright with his fingerprints on top.

BAM BE LIKE . . .

Redbone was something else

MANNNNNNNN
she kept me on my toes, boy
she caught me cheating on her
drove me to ole girl house

& said

"tell that bitch you coming home"

BAM BEHIND BARS AFTER BEATING A MAN WITH A BASEBALL BAT

"I let him live,   didn't I?"

REDBONE REFLECTION

i.

yo, read my palm
let us find wisdom in the wine
in time, the wine will make us lovewise

i am a product of the dirt, love
the love produces dirt, creates we
we create destructive circles in cycles:
a cesarean in reverse

an addiction to addicts ain't as sexy as it seems
children born in this kind of desert
are always thirsty

ii.

give me my mother's bone structure

& her gap tooth slaughter

give me her spine—Redbone got a spine for the world

give me a vertebra for him to lose his religion in

give him a way to find his lost self   back home

a man without a god is:
a bear trap
a glorious disaster
a sublime hemorrhage

They all leave. You learn. The cul de sac don't hold no one too long. At least now you know how it's gonna be. This is it. All the brown grass where the tree stands bare. The balding brown grows heavy. Like your sigh. Like your mother's face with age. Like everyone's voice when they say *amen.* Like everyone's voice when they say nothing. Nothing is heavy. Nothing sounds like a glass pipe / a good song. Stratford, Oak Park, Helen, and Poplar. To the left, where your cousin died. To the right, where you mother dies. On the red porch, all that light. They gone leave, you learn. Pelican Bay. Vacaville. Stockton. Folsom. Citadel full of "bad" men. So close to dead men, you don't even write. Don't want to confuse what your blood speaks. Look at the sky instead. Look at the book instead. Drop the glass. Crush it slow. Clip your tongue when speaking of the gone. Don't speak of the gone. Just be. Check out this dark pit. Ain't it home enough?

LITTLE DEATHS

if the day unfolds before a lover speaks your name
shout it from the rafters of your cheeks
sprinkle it over your steel cut oatmeal
stir it into your coffee, this unhollowing prayer
       slow   slow   slow   name   slow   slow

it is only a Saturday
and church is congregating with each breath
your lover sleeps like a sermon
like a body that worships only one name
you walk like that light is yours

if the day unfolds into the hands of two lovers
       they walk like there is no one watching
you study them
if you are lucky your hand is its own warmth
   if the sun setting unfolds into a day like this

let it swallow the cold from your lips
let it lengthen each little death

****

MAMA'S SUGAR

there is a gun / the color don't matter / you hold it loose:
    unimpressed / heavy door / heavy pistol
there is a gun / the color of your mama's sugar / the color of
    your grandma's abandoned eyes

BONE GARDEN

after Natalie Diaz

in this garden / this cadaver jar / this head of hurt &
remembering /the head is only a heavy-handed metaphor for
negro / for missing father for steel scriptures haunt my nest
of cracks/   America is the culprit/ & no one cares/in this
jar — this bone/this cone of mayhem/ This eggshell-colored
chaos/this splintered husk of prison bar frenzy — swinging
like a basement party reggae room/no one dances / here my
glare is my only weapon / my father is a fire bouncing from
the rind / no one cares about my missing roof/how all us
seeds be longing for / a rain free sky / — even our clay is a
prayer in chorus

There was that one time I thought I could recover my soul from the heat of a random man's mouth. It must've been on the dance floor in San Francisco after I left my high school sweetheart in search of myself. He had a way of not looking at me when I talked to him. Or looking through me when I talked to him. Almost like the time I thought my father, home fresh from prison, could never hear me clearly, unless I spoke to him *real real* fast. Sped through his sentences like a runaway vehicle, in the back of a vehicle, I spilled every fact I stored in my memory, waiting for his attention to return. Until his hands sliced through the air like a switch. Until his open palm landed on my mouth like firecracker. Closed me shut *real* good. So there I was, on the dance floor, forgetting about the man that asked me to choose him over poetry. Forgetting about the man that only had rough hands to father me. A trick he learned from his father. A trick my grandfather learned from his country.

Across the bridge, my daughter is sleeping on her stomach. A pacifier in her mouth as my grandmother's television light tenderly strokes her face. I don't remember how to remember the little things. Just the order of must have beens. I remember returning home to rinse his touch from me. Remember I changed my daughter's diaper and lie her in bed beside me. Can't forget she will wake in search of milk in five hours. Can't seem to unmemorize the way this wake served as a search of devotion three years after. Which leads me back to an Oakland apartment. This new man, released from jail and reminiscent of the most familiar hunt. I keep men like him at a distance. But I ask for his hands on my face, him in my mouth, his hands against my throat—searching for a piece of earth to hold onto.

BREAKING ALPHA ALMIGHTY

at dinner I hallucinated   your heart
perched on the table   next
to the salad bowl and breadsticks
                in wait
Our love almighty   bookmarked
for a place   of glare of red and safe
how coal and smudged it became
            a glint gone in your brown eyes
A black man with eyes   like yours
            is a nuisance
A man with eyes like yours
can steal anything
from women like me

        My daughter has your eyes

        ***

You refuse to respond
        you man of many silences
you man with several tongues and no spine
        you are why I left California
why I slept with another man
        and called him asylum
I blame your mother for your brown eyes
        and body full of abandon

she taught you the fable of   a woman's place
          she encouraged you to be ravaged by silence
when it came to men   she was a mouse
          when it came to me   she was a jackal
and your name is the winter I can never rid my cold skin
          most days   I wish   you were dead
so I could teach my daughter
          how to correctly mourn a memory

***

I am a good person.
I am flawed like Jonah.
I am tried like Job.
I praise the Lord.
I am here because of Him.
You are gone now
Because you do not know a woman's place.
So I go to church.
I pray you repent.
I pray for you like a harvest
        prays for locusts' kiss
I don't want to hear your poems.
I will never call
I don't know who you are anymore.
And now my daughter doesn't know who I am.
It is your fault.
This is all your fault.
Repent. Repent.
Praise the Lord.

***

A Black woman with eyes like yours
      is always prey
The place where women are respected is a fleeting one
       and the world is ready to devour my daughter
It is why I taught her to walk like me
       head above the smoke   arms boa constrict around books
She has the kind of eyes that stir the sidewalks   dizzy
       she hasn't said your name in 90 days
I stopped loving you long before the dinner
       spilled with wine glasses and two pink lines
The day you let another woman braid your hair
       an act of wishbone sorcery
Too late, I was already a bonfire of bones
       a smoke cloud signaling farewell
       a slow sift trampling free
       amidst the soot and your filthy name

BABY MAMA LAMENT

If every
thing is a given
I return your silence
Her last name
Her last utterance
Your fear of a forever
I give all those heavy undoings
  back

MONSOON

he move like water;
a monsoon man
& you be a boat
—the smallest kind—
of woman still afraid
the tenor will break
your everything.

MUSING(S)

& I keep   staring   while he   stay
looking   at me   look at him   he thinkin'
'bout: what the hell he know   I'm   gone
take him through   still   he love me   so
like most Blk men   he   love   like a wound
he say the words w/his eyes   let his hands go
soft   hold my faith   like a breakable thing
he right   my heart is a river crashing
in a mason jar   &   his tongue
is a stubborn boat that can't let   go

they stole the car. you gat ready. you turn into your father so quick. the cul de sac calls you out your name when you sleep. you wake with a séance crust in your eyes. they all know when you got a wrong decision to make. word get along like wind. that's how the block know everything. yea, Stratford know. yea, Poplar know. street names colored in tree sap sermons. maybe that's why the sun so hot. or why the water so ice. that's why the drug boys whistle. that's why you sleep late. that's why you skip breakfast. that's why your knees jerk and brush against the gat silent in your lap. your fingers slide against the life drainer. then your fingers don't move at all. you begin to rap your knuckles against the door. the screen just'a singing like you an old friend. black black marbles peek out: *they ain't here. they ain't got it. they gone.*

you almost smile. they can't see your hands. but they know you real.

your gaped haunt opening. and now they scared to hear you laugh.

BAM BE LIKE . . .

don't put no gangbanger in here with me
    Why you shaking your head?
don't put no funny boys up in here neither
    Why you shaking your head?
send me a letter
    Why you shaking your head?
don't send me no letter . . .
    . . . Then I don't have no daughter

Redbone live across the street from the mall now
She used to have a BMW, she used to have a husband,
She used to own a house,
With kids in the front room & a crack habit
That got too big to hide in a valley's cul de sac

She say she clean now
She say she top heavy & in God's image
She say *"we blessed, tho, we sure are blessed*
to be here"—Coco's descendants

She say she live by the 99 cent store now
She say she need the Obama phone
She say, I live by the mall, everything is around here
She say *"I'm good with that"*

MY MOTHER, REDBONE

ain't no wonder my curves curse a song
BLACK girls be full of dirt
carnation milk and tidal waves

my mother is a Redbone,
she split into twos for her lovers
birthed a trifecta of globes for them fools

my mother ain't never pray with me.

she ain't no heathen
just a *firetongue* slow*crawl* woman
who taught me to hiss my simmer s l o w

my mother, a mighty tool
a firestack, smoking—
a bow missing every arrow
like an itchy trigger finger

her cackle break through the wind like law
she ain't never been afraid of a gut check

and I am her greatest weapon
she sock my name to the sky
I smile like every BLACK girl should

redbone girls get tough quick or
get gone quicker
she sip her simmer hiss talk s l o w

every BLACK girl wonder what the wind feel like
without her dark skin
tug loose like nightfall rain

don't speak 'bout paper bags
Redbone grumble   you mines
all BLACK all tidal waves
you a pretty ole downpour

my mother ain't never pray with me

ain't no need askin' for forgiveness
for what the D'vil done already let loose.

REDBONE & A STRETCH OF HIGHWAY

He got a motorcycle, it's loud,
if you ride it up Greenhaven Avenue
it make your whole body tingle.

He got a gun & He smell sour.
He stomp around Redbone's new house.
Like he owns it.

Redbone ain't porcelain but close
she wait for him to say words
that form sentences. He do.

But when He don't, He just sit
in a grey cloud of sizzle & steel.

Redbone sit there, too. Waiting
for something to happen.

KEROSENE LITANY

I wish I could break
All the chains holding me
—*Nina Simone*

today
i am a Black woman in america
& i am singing a melody ridden lullaby
It sounds like the gentrification of a brooklyn stoop
the bodega and laundromat burned down on the corner
the people each the corner
lock & key their chromosomes
a note of ash & inquiry on their tongue

today
i am a Black woman in a hopeless state
i will apply for financial aid and food stamps
with the same mouth i spit poems from
i will ask the angels of a creative god to lessen the storm
& i will beg for forgiveness if ever i curse
the rising dawn

today
i am a Black woman in a body of coal
i am combustible and no one cares knows my name
i am a nameless fury, i am a blues scratched from
the throat of ms. Nina—i am always angry

i am always a bumble hive of hello

today
i am a cold country, a certain storm,
a heat swell & audacity of being woman

today
i am a woman, a brown and black &
brew woman dreaming of a freedom

today
i am a mother, and my country is burning
& i forget how to flee from such a flamboyant
backdraft
—i'm too in awe of how ravishing i look
        ablaze

IF WE PRAISE

the names of
our fallen

We lift the broken
with our light

We praise their names
        & the hands that write
Praise the mouth that speaks
Praise the truth that soars
        from the spine of the most nimble creatures

Praise us creatures
        & our immodest fragility
Praise the humility
The learned spaces
The space that dissolves
& births the wind
Praise the wind
        & the storms that change course

Praise the creatures born & reborn
Praise the boom bap split silence shattered
Praise the fragmented bodies & heavy breathing like rain
Praise the rain

Feeding our hearts & homes & leaves

Praise the green

Praise the Black

Praise the bullet breaking brown flesh like fruit

Praise the fruit

Praise the stomachs & minds unfed

Praise the hungry

Praise the God in everything

Praise yourself

Your own flesh

Sinewy boundless overweight glorious & alive

Praise the life

Praise the durable love

Praise our sovereign journey

Praise the destruction

How it reminds us that ribs heal

    & purpled lips return perfect & pointing towards the sun

Praise the burial

Praise the new day & the healing

    Praise the repetition

The times it will take us to remember we are beautiful

    we are beautiful

    we are beautiful

    & worth the stretched breath of the unimagined & unseen

Praise the nightmares we've endured

The salt we've tasted in our release
Praise the divine living
& our voices reaching towards the sky
singing our own name

BIRTH RITE

Bam's first daughter
wears the errant crown
of the son he always wanted

she s t r e t c h across
the blacktop   the sky pulls
at her jaws until her lips pout betrayal

she growls
like him they say
so she decides
it is her favorite sound

CROWNED

^^^^^^

If the mouth is a house
Then most days I am homeless

My Mama taught me   ____
women are loved best when silent

Once I leaned into a man's shoulder blade
          ____

I haven't found my tongue ever since

I hear my father is a dream boat

It is no wonder I am afraid of the sea
          ____

Each wave carries a sound I don't have the courage to carry

^^^^^^

If the mouth has four walls
Then is the roof a spotless wonder?

^^^^^^

My Mama fetched her voice box for a pipe once//I've been
    scared of smoke ever since

^^^^^^^

No mouth no cave no casket no shadow

^^^^^^

My mouth harbors love like a well
Except most days the container is brittle
I've been taught to fear large bodies of water

& boats
& men w/the collarbone of a man i can't remember but will
    always relocate the familiar
hum

^^^^^^^   _____

mommy mouth screamed at a gun twice
Each shot siren sung like an air raid or a prison break or a black
    man's back

                                ____

I am always concerned w/my tone
San Quentin children learn they place
In the limestone

somewhere;
my father got a skeleton awake & swaying

I'm still afraid to go home
I've learned to live amongst a commune of
ghosts

Each ghost got a special something
& remind me of sin
                    ^^^^   ____

Where all the women talk   real loud
Let men marry them or not
Hit them or not
Leave them then come back
Year passed and skin sagged
Locks unchained

^^^^^^^^^^

Mouths unhinged
& swinging hello to any two-bit hustler w/swagger

No matter if he arrive w/another woman's scent tucked in his
    collarbone

                    ^^^^

My mommy used to sing to me
I've no proof
— but my spirit whispers sunsilk memoir in my dreams

Anytime I hear a horn scuttle across the dusty room
I think:
this sound smells like my mother

It's the best kind of sleep

way after dusk

well before I wake   ^^^^^^
w/a bullet between my teeth

THE CYCLE

Break womb
Break glass
        Break
        Break
    Break
Break

    Red cries
    Red plans
    Red sighs
    Break

Bam lies
Bam knows
Bam leaves
Break

    Red lives
    Red laughs
    Red learns
    Break

Red open
Red wide
Red broken
Break

Red runs
Red hides
Red unpacks
Break

Red runs
Red unpacks
Red hides
Break

Red sun
Red shines
Red loves
Break

Red believes
Red holds
Red regrets
Break

Red weeps
Red recovers
Red conceals
Break

Red baby
Red husband
Red lonely
Break

Red lonely
Red baby
Red leaves
Break

Red lost
Red found
Red footing
Break

Red falls
Red smoke
Red lies
Break

Red beat
Red down
Red fly y y y y
Crack

Crack

Crack

Cra/ck

DEAR DAUGHTER

a Black woman with eyes like ours
    always be prey
****

this kin   this stone toss family   this kin this death of
choice   this choice of addiction
this kin addicted to dying   this Black death that smells like
home   this home
this heart has no home   this heart found a home in
Brooklyn   in airports   in a little girl's smile   in the halo
of displacement   in a little bit better   it will
all be better   if I could just have this home   this
house   this man that i love   this love i can't hold   this man
that i need   this life i can't hold   this want   this now   this
here   this Black   that I can't separate from my skin   this
bone   attached to the breaking sunrise of this   smile   this
root of all evil   this woman   this evil   this woman   this
God   this evil to think myself evil   this God   this
evil   to think myself   anything less than
        woman:
        this Bermuda
        this Stonehenge
        this temple
        this flesh
        & this fat
        this sister
        this lover
        this wife
this *here*   be more than jump off   this be more
        than your free milk

this be your mother's lonely   this Black girl   this
bricklayer   this woman
that can't forget   how to kiss like shadows   how to smile
like crypt keepers how to pray like a whisper   how to forget
where she came from   where she came from?   from a gutter
of a woman   & a jawbreaker of a man   this hammer head
love   sits on my chest
this   crunch   this   crush   this   sound   of   breakable
things   this   worthless   thing this   worthwhile
thing   this breath is worthwhile   this hurt is worth
now   this now is worth tomorrow   this tomorrow ain't
even here yet   this concrete crack tomorrow   this glass
chipped tomorrow   this morning song of good   this Billie
Holiday heartbreak *good*
    this Nina Simone *feel good*   tomorrow's full of good

    this bloody pulp

this

    this

ACKNOWLEDGMENTS

Thank you for picking up this book. For holding this book. Or maybe just picking it up and tossing it. Or deep reading until these pages wave into a visual soundscape. All of those moments are still proof of life. And so I am thankful for living. I am thankful for my mother, who chose my father. For their making of me. For their parents, whose love made them. For the lineage of survival and soar.

I am thankful for the readers and friends, comrades and mentors, students turned teachers: I am only here because you took a chance on the wind in me. You took a chance on me when no one else would even look in my dark direction. Thank you for seeing such light in darkness and such humor in the litany and such glitter in the thrill of seeing your work tremor the waters endlessly.

My mother, Ellaine Toni. You are a righteous woman. You have taught me to move with the same soundness and consistency. You have taught me love and forgiveness, friendship and faith. I am because of you. I love you.

Jive Poetic & Amari, my light. Adam Falkner, Ocean Vuong, Marwa Helal, Nicole Sealey, Terrance Hayes, Camonghne Felix, Hanif Abdurraqib, Hala Alyan, Jon Sands, Jennifer Falu, Charlotte Sheedy & Sheedy Lit Agency, Tim Seibles, Patricia Smith, Jacqueline Woodson, Cristin O'Keefe Aptowicz, Sarah Kay, Caroline Rothstein, Tongo Eisen-Martin, Ana Paula & Anya of Blueflower Arts, Jason Reynolds, Christine Platt, Rico Frederick, Sofia Snow, Ayana Walker, Whitney Greenaway, Ross Gay, the freshest team at Liveright: Gina Iaquinta and Zeba Arora.

Academy of American Poets, Yes Yes Books, Button Poetry, Cave Canem Foundation, Baldwin for the Arts, Urban Word NYC, Ode to Babel, Rauschenberg Residency, Writing Downton (Las Vegas, Nevada), John F. Kennedy Center for the Performing Arts, & Lincoln Center for the Performing Arts.

I am grateful to my ancestors who made this collection possible.